# AN INTRODU(

# CLASSICAL YANG STYLE

# TAI CHI AND QIGONG

## The Ultimate Beginners Guide

BY

PETER NEWTON

**SECOND EDITION**

Published By China Bridge Publications
68 Llanrhos Road, Penrhyn Bay
Llandudno, Conwy.
LL30 3HY.




Printed and Bound in Great Britain By
Anthony Rowe Ltd, Bumper`s Farm
Chippenham, Wiltshire.
SN14 6LH.



ISBN  0  9533  2041  3

# CONTENTS

# CHAPTER ONE

# INTRODUCTION TO AUTHOR

## PETER NEWTON.
## Chief Instructor of the China Bridge Centre.

Welcome to the world of traditional Chinese health and martial arts, I will be both guide and instructor on this introductory tour of in my opinion the most graceful and interesting systems of health and self defence. I have had the honour of training with some of the best masters in the world today namely: Master Chu King Hung, Master Michael Tse, Master Yang Jwing Ming and recently attended a seminar held by Grand Master Chen Xiao Wang. My accumulated training under Masters Chu, Tse and Yang amounts to 20 years.

In the early nineties I travelled to London to perform my skills to the technical panel of the; "Tai Chi Union for Great Britain." And have since represented them in Wales and Chester as their Regional Officer. This is a seriously growing and expanding organisation, set up to ensure all registered instructors are of the highest possible standard, having been formally trained in a recognised system.

Prior to taking up Tai Chi Chuan in the early eighties, I dabbled in Karate, Wing Chun Kung Fu and Aikido, none of which I found suited me. It was when I saw an old Chinese gentleman in his nineties in a televised documentary on China, who was moving with such grace, flexibility and power, that it brought me to the edge of my seat. The narrator explained that he was a master of an ancient health and martial art system he called Tai Chi Chuan.

I was astounded as to how a man of his age could perform movements that were beyond me, a person some seventy years his junior. Immediately I realised that this is what I had been searching for and

1

therefore, decided to look for teachers in my local area. A short time later I discovered a Kung Fu school that taught Wing Chun and Tai Chi based in North Wales. This training lasted just over a year until I had to leave due to breaking a bone in my foot. However, during my stay I was taught Wing Chun Sparring, both semi and full contact (which caused the damage to my foot) and three Tai Chi forms of barehand, broadsword and staff. Also, I was introduced to what I now recognise was Chin Na (grasp and control skills ).

This seriously wetted my appetite, so after my injury had healed, I received information that there was a traditional teacher of Tai Chi in the Chester area, who was reputed to be of high calibre. I soon located Sifu (Teacher) Dave Evans who was the Northwest representative of Master Chu King Hung one of the senior students of Grandmaster Yang Sau Chung, at that time the current head of the; "Yang" family, from whom the style got its name.

Thus began my training in Classical Yang Style Tai Chi and after a short period of time, I was introduced to Master Chu. Thereafter I trained weekly with Sifu Dave in his Chester class and with Master Chu on a one to one basis.

In 1998 I became a full time professional instructor and haven't looked back since then. Now into my third year I am pleased to say the demand is still steadily increasing, which I'm doing my best to service. Conscious however, not to take too much on otherwise health and prosperity may suffer.

# CHAPTER TWO

# INTRODUCTION

I decided to produce this book after receiving many requests from my students, especially those who had recently joined with no previous Tai Chi experience. They felt it would be useful to have at their disposal an easy to follow guide and introduction to Tai Chi and Qigong. To be used as an ongoing reference manual to the key Tai Chi postures in their choreographed sequence. Showing direction and location of limb positions by way of simple instructions, supported by photographs.

I was also asked to detail my own training background which I have done in chapter one. The rest of the book will comprise of special Qigong (Energy Exercise) drills that prepare the body and mind for Tai Chi training (see chapter six). These are fundamental to the correct teaching and practice of the art and are viewed by the Chinese as being the foundation to support and produce quality Tai Chi.

The style of Tai Chi I will be demonstrating in chapter seven is known as; "Classical Yang," and is generally accepted as the most commonly known and practiced of the; "Five Families," or what we in the western world would call the market leaders. The four others being Wu, Chen, Woo and Sun. Whilst each one differs slightly from one another they all follow the same fundamental principles, which are known as; the "Classics" (see chapter ten). These are the ancient texts based on the original teachings and maxims of the reputed founder of the art Chang San Feng (see chapter three). That have been handed down from master to student as the instruction manual for correct practice.

The special 39 posture Tai Chi Form in this book is a shorter version of the Original Classical Long Form (108 posture). Which, I have found to be more acceptable to newcomers, who find it difficult to digest the Long Form from day one. When students have completed the first form they are usually fired up for the full "Classical." Made easier to learn by virtue of the fact, all the Short Form postures are repeated in the Long Form.

3

The sequence of photographs shown in this book, correspond to the Short Form showing snap shots of the main postures only. I have purposely left out the intermediate linking postures, as it is impossible to learn them from a book. Instead I suggest you locate a qualified teacher who has been formally trained in the Original Authentic Yang Family Style.

This new edition includes an extra eight chapters, designed to cover the vast array of material necessary for beginners to grasp the principles of these enigmatic arts. Including: a much enhanced explanation of what Tai Chi and Qigong are, by evaluating their Taoist roots and beginnings. An appreciation of their fundamental benefits. And their interface with Feng Shui to help you understand the organic nature of these arts.

"Experiences" pokes a little gentle fun at ourselves highlighting our uniqueness in how we all differ from one another. I also make one or two bold statements regarding our failings as a nation in looking after ourselves especially in adult life.

Another new chapter discusses meditation and its benefits. Something I think should be taught in school to children so that they develop into earthed and centred adults, thus creating a more peaceful society to live in.

The Tai Chi Classics, 13 Postures and Taoist Meditation chapters are all written with beginners in mind, however like most Tai Chi manuals the written word comes alive only when you practice the art, with a qualified teacher on hand to explain the intricacies a book cannot deliver.

Finally I have included a chapter called; "Questions and Answers," that is designed to save wear and tear of my vocal chords. As I've lost count how many times I'm asked the same questions every week. Thankfully all I have to say now is... 'read chapter twelve.'

Practicing Tai Chi and Qigong must form part of a daily regime as it will improve your quality of life on both emotional and physical levels. Which is what the Chinese call Tai Chi ie: when a person acquires harmony with life and nature their Yin and Yang are said to be balanced.

I therefore dedicate this book to you the student, may it help you gain the wisdom and enrich your life in the way it has mine, by protecting you on this earth journey.

# CHAPTER THREE

# WHAT ARE

# TAI CHI AND QIGONG?

To understand Tai Chi and Qigong you must first consider Taoism, which is their source and inspiration. It is a way of life that in it's extreme would be difficult to follow in our modern day. However, find yourself a secluded island blessed with good Feng Shui and I suppose anything is possible.

Taoism is a philosophical way of life practiced by Taoists who are the followers of the; "Way," and how does one describe the Way? Lao Tsu a famous Taoist sage who lived approximately 2500 years ago questions in his book of; "Virtue and the Way," (Tao Te Ching): 'He who speaks of the Tao, does not know it, and he who knows it does not speak of it.' So, how do you explain that which is indescribable? Suffice to say, I think what he means is, in order to explain the Tao, you would need to see it and in order to see it you must look for it. But, if you are an intrinsic part of the Tao itself in the first place, consequently you can't look for what you already are.

From a philosophical point of view we can learn something from this, for example: how many of us constantly search for answers to our physical and or emotional problems, we try one thing, lose interest then try another, but always not quite achieving the stimulus or results that we sought. We look outward for the answers without realising they lie within, blaming everyone but ourselves for our follies.

The Tao redirects our attention inward to face our inner demons and progressively remove them from our being. Once cleansed you are at a state the Chinese masters call; "empty." Where Qi can flow throughout the body unrestricted and your spirit (Shen) is free from its earthly shackles. The Chinese describe Taoists as Huang Lao, which means

5

students of the respected folklaw figures, Huang Ti (The Yellow Emperor) and Lao Tzu. Huang Ti who lived around 2600BC was said to be responsible for a golden age in China's history and is regarded as the founder of Chinese civilisation as the first ruler of the empire.

He is most famous for being the instigator of the first fully detailed book on traditional Chinese medicine, known as the "Nei Ching" which translates to; "Classic Book of Internal Medicine." Through exhaustive work and experimentation he is reputed to have discovered the secret of immortality. The Nei Ching is so profound, it still forms the bedrock of Chinese medical practices and his influence in the forging of Chinese culture puts him in pole position as one of China's most respected deities.

According to to legend, Huang Ti lived in the era in Chinese history known as; the "Five Emperor Sages" (2852 - 2579BC). Where spiritual cultivation reached it's highest state and their refined life force vibrations enabled them to; "Communication With The Gods." This cultivation of body and spirit to attain the Tao or Way is the primary goal of the Taoist, who seeks to immortalise the Shen (Spirit), which they affectionately describe as; "Returning to the Source."

These enlightened Taoists are accredited with the invention , discovery and practice of: Silk Weaving, Alchemy, Cosmology, Traditional Medicine including; Acupuncture, Moxibism, Homoeopathy and a therapeutic health science that comprises: Massage, Yogic Exercise (Qigong), Meditation, and were the primary influencers in the creation of Tai Chi Chuan.

To practice Tai Chi and Qigong correctly and therefore fully benefit from their rejuvenative properties, you do not have to become a Taoist recluse locked away from society in some remote mountain region. But, you do need to ascribe to at least some their key maxims or doctrines. For example; you must learn to understand what they mean by cultivation and nourishment of; the "Three Treasures which I shall now briefly describe. The first of the "Treasures" is the Ching (Sexual Essence), they discovered by limiting the release of sexual fluids the body would store this conserved sexual energy. Which through Qigong practice was converted into the high vibration "Spiritual Energy," stored in the "Sky Eye" located at the centre of the forehead.

The next Treasure is the Shen (Spirit), nature sees to it that a healthy body and mind nourishes the Shen and when we feel good our Spirits are raised, prompting a comment like; 'Your in high spirits.' The feeling of wellbeing that envelopes us at times of joy and happiness, is this spiritual energy and if sustained can fuse the body and mind into a strong and robust union.

The last Treasure is the Qi (Vital Energy), generally represented by the breath which in my opinion is the most important of the three, as it's impact is immediate. For example; sustained low or high spirits or excessive sexual activity won't seriously damage your health in the short term (over a period of years however, the internal organs will weaken). Whereas withholding the breath for more than six minutes will kill you.

So, the Taoists found when they regulated their sexual behaviour and the breath, the body's ability to store Qi increased dramatically, which in turn had a tonic like effect on the spirit. Those who achieved the balance between the Three Treasures were said to have; 'the strength of a lumberjack, the pliability of a young child and the peace of mind of a sage.'

They also understood body engineering in relation to posture and how it should interface with gravitational force. This omnipresent force can be made to work in your favour, but beware, choose the path of ignorance and she will bend you over and disfigure you.

The fact that Taoists are known for their hermit like life style, indicates they did not enjoy living in the limelight, as it would have distracted them from their ultimate goal of enlightenment. They discovered it was only possible through the elimination of stress and all its symptoms from their lives. And when you compare conditions then to now, it is understandable how they could retreat to the mountains and live off the land without meeting another human soul.

Now let us probe a little deeper to unlock more of the secrets and mystic that surround Tai Chi and Qigong. Which I'm sure one day science will be able to sensibly explain and recognize as something that is real and tangible, not dreams or flights of fancy conjured up by an overactive imagination.

The first and most fundamental thing to understand is that you must, like the Taoists "Cultivate and Nurture" the Qi from the outset. This means serious review of your life style and the setting up of a regular training programme that must be strictly adhered to. True cultivation comes from regular practice of Qigong, Tai Chi, Taoist Meditation and the application and implementation of the philosophical wisdom that surrounds these arts. So, what is the difference between Tai Chi and Qigong? A simple way of explaining is; Qigong supplies the Qi and Tai Chi circulates it.

## Qigong.

Translates to mean; "Energy Exercise or Skill," it is by nature non martial yet as I'll explain a little later it has a hard side to it's character. Qigong is classified as the foundation block of Tai Chi and as Master Chu once said; 'It is the fuel that fires the engine of the vehicle which is Tai Chi.'

There are three ways to practice this unique therapeutic art, one is standing, the second is sitting and the third is moving. In standing you strike an upright or squatting posture (see chapter nine for a detailed account) and firmly plant your feet on the ground. By correctly aligning your spine and limbs the key acupuncture points are encouraged to open and absorb Heaven and Earth Qi in a more efficient manner. The whole thing being driven by a more efficient lung function due to your improved posture.

Sitting Qigong can be practiced sat on a chair with your feet flat on the floor or sat on the floor in cross leg, half lotus, or full lotus position, the key maxim being to keep the spine upright. (see chapter nine for details). Sitting Qigong is principally concerned with developing Qi circulation in the arms and torso. When you have accomplished a strong and smooth flow of Qi around the torso this lays a foundation for; "Large or Grand Circulation." Derived from standing and moving Qigong, from which Tai Chi can be generally classified. This being one of the lesser but still important goals of the art, where the Qi can freely circulate around the whole body.

Moving Qigong entails applying the same internal training methods adopted in sitting and standing methods, within the postures that flow into each other, in a choreographed pattern with nimble footwork at their base. A good example of this can be seen in the system of exercise known as; "Dayan Qigong," which imitates the graceful movements and gestures of the Wild Goose. The flowing posture sequence opens up the meridians and major acupuncture points, which clears away blockages allowing Qi to circulate throughout the body.

Like Tai Chi, moving Qigong carries strong therapeutic properties being beneficial to sufferers of a variety of complaints and conditions (see chapter eleven, Health Benefits). Qigong in general is designed to work with the body in a manner that totally harmonises with it's natural rhythms. In addition it encourages the natural anatomical motorisation of the body to stay at all times in line with gravitational force. Combined with the special breathing skills it truly becomes an "internal art." In that it works in conjunction the external physical movements, thus creating complete unification of the internal with the external, represented by the symbols of Yin and Yang respectively.

Qigong has different facets to its practice that may be separated into three categories: The first is Medical, which I have briefly touched on above but cover in depth in chapter eleven. Those on this path tend to be people already with physical or emotional problems, it also attracts the "Healers" within our society. The second is Spiritual, which involves the quest to achieve enlightenment, some say this is the true way, but I question whether in today's world with all its distractions and pressures we will ever reach the dizzy heights of the old masters.

The foundation for spiritual training involves many regular hours of practice with the aim of detaching you from all "External" influences. So that you can focus inward to cultivate the spirit leading to a heightened awareness. Taoists talk of the spirit ultimately returning to it's source, where it is welcomed back to the Tao, regarded as the root and origin of all life.

In a religious sense I guess it is the equivalent of entering into the kingdom of heaven. In order to follow this spiritual path you would have to become extremely self sufficient and live in isolation from your fellow man. Or you could join a Taoist or Buddhist monastic order where you you be positively encouraged to achieve your goal. In reality however, the best I suggest we are able to achieve is a level where we are able to peer through the misty window of the enlightened for a glimpse of the riches behind it's shimmering veil.

The third is Martial Qigong, practiced as a form of internal and external body conditioning by most Chinese martial arts schools, to toughen and protect the body from blows received in combat. This method is categorised as being; "Hard Qigong." Thus described for obvious reasons, whereas medical and spiritual Qigong are classed as; "Soft" styles. The soft style goes back to the root of the art, whilst hard style was reputed to have been conceived around 500 AD. Where it is recorded an Indian monk by the name of Da Mo (also known as Bodhidarma), travelled to China on invitation of the emperor to preach Buddhism at his court. Having probably all he could stomach of the hustle and bustle of court life, he left and headed for the more serene and peaceful atmosphere of the Shaolin temple, which at that time had not embraced the martial arts into it's doctrines.

Upon arrival he was saddened to see fellow monks in relatively poor health and felt obliged to rectify their situation. Unfortunately for the monks however, they had to wait for nine years before he brought the answer to their prayers. That is how long he is reputed to have incarcerated himself in a nearby cave, to contemplate on the answer to their plight. His unbelievable sacrifice bore fruits, for from this cell of enlightenment he produced two incredible texts written with; the "Guidance Of The Gods." These texts contained details of therapeutic practices that not only dramatically improved the health of the monks, but also gave them the means to excel in the martial arts.

At that time Shaolin priests were easy prey to bandits as they walked to neighbouring towns or villages for provisions, or to conduct religious festivals by offering blessings to the people. No doubt some may have even been killed, which is why they decided to incorporate self defence training into their daily regimes. The instruments Do Mo had given them became absorbed into their martial arts training. And such was their impact, that to this day Shaolin Monks are revered throughout the world for their incredible and almost super human powers.

Da Mo had written and personally taught them; the "Yi Jin Jing," (Muscle Tendon Changing Classic) and; the "Xi Ji Jing," (Marrow Brain Washing Classic). Briefly, Yi Jin Jing teaches special exercises that brings an abundance of Qi to the muscles and tendons, stimulating them to operate at maximum efficiency thus creating natural body armour. The Xi Jin Jing however, operates more internally in that it is designed to strengthen the bone marrow and thus the bones themselves. It also directs Qi to the internal organs, and especially the brain, which is said to be "Washed Clean" to enable the priests to access enlightenment much sooner by virtue of this knowledge.

These two Qigong systems are linked to a martial Qigong known as; "Iron Shirt." Which is a true descriptive reflection of the results of regular practice of these arts. Whilst there are numerous variations depending on the style practiced, two of the most famous carry the mystical names of: Ermie Seven Stars and Heavenly River Monastery.

To watch someone performing any of the above would leave you thinking them somewhat bizzare. Especially when you witness them sucking and blowing air in and out, sounding like a steam train. following this up with half an hour of almost masochistic self punishment, as they beat their whole body repeatedly with a bundle of thick wire strands, toughening skin, bone and muscle in the process. However, the end results seem to justify their efforts, as they do actually develop a body that can withstand immense punishment, that would probably kill or maim the likes of you or I. It is my fervent belief that one day in the not too distant future, science will have the technology to logically explain how our Qi can be utilised like this. So that it can be positively nurtured to help heal those whom, would otherwise suffer in the void where treatment using conventional medicine ends.

## Tai Chi Chuan.

Tai Chi Chuan translates to mean Grand Ultimate Boxing or Fist, which it's name infers, was originated as a highly respected martial art. It will always be a mystery as to whether it was created knowing it's therapeutic essence, or simply as a martial art that combined Qigong science and body engineering, forging perfection in motion and power.

The reputed founder of this art, a gentleman by the name of Chang San Feng, did in fact have the necessary credentials to combine the two. He was a Taoist monk who lived sometime between the twelfth and fourteenth centuries AD. Having turned his back on society he took to the mountains in search of enlightenment and as legend states, he began his education with the monks of the Shaolin Temple. Here they taught him humility, patience, determination and their philosophical wisdom thought to be essential for those who choose the path to enlightenment. In addition to this he became an accomplished master of Shaolin Chuan which is their unique and special style of boxing.

After mastering all he could, he is then said to have left and moved to Wu Dang mountain, where he reputedly conceived the idea of Tai Chi Chuan. By combining his original skills of a Qigong practitioner and acupuncturist with his Shaolin training a uniquely balanced system of

11

martial and health arts emerged. Over the ensuing centuries this special art became coveted by the five families or clans namely: the Chen's, Yang's, Woo's, Sun's and Wu's. Whose untold dedication to research and develop the art has provided the yard-stick from which we, the current generation, merely scratch the surface of the incredible achievements attributed to these revered old masters. In chapter eleven I explore the health benefits of Tai Chi in great detail and therefore intend to mainly discuss it's martial aspect here.

What is it then that makes Tai Chi stand out amongst the host of other Chinese martial arts ? The simple answer is it's; "Nei" or inner aspect. Most of the other styles rely on muscle power to deliver their message which is therefore categorised as primary. Whereas although Tai Chi appreciates the importance of good and healthy toned muscle, it is classed as secondary to the tendons and inner Qi power called; "Jing." The muscles still provides the body armour, but it is the tendons fired by "Taoist Breathing" that delivers this power, creating a whip like release of energy called; "Fa Jing" which means; "Explosive Power." In order to work effectively the pulse of this energy must be released with lightening speed and focused to hit one of the many "Cavities" or "Sensitive Acupuncture Points" mapped out on the body.

The result from an accurately placed strike can be quite catastrophic for the recipient for example: a blow to the Ching Men or Liver Cavity, can cause irreversible damage to that organ, that could potentially kill it's victim. This sort of knowledge in the wrong hands is very dangerous and it was for this reason, the Tai Chi families only taught this; "Dim Mak" or "Death Blow," to direct family or trusted friends.

In order to fully appreciate martial Tai Chi you must learn; the "Form," which is a series of choreographed postures within which, lie all it's hidden treasures. The late Grand Master Yang Sau Chung head of the Yang family said; 'You must examine every movement, even down to the subtle motion of the fingers.' All the angles, directions and locations for punching, chopping, prodding, bumping, grasping and breaking are found within the form. Even if you never have to use the skills to defend yourselves, it is still a fascinating voyage of discovery to unravel it's mysteries.

At the core of martial Tai Chi sits the deceptive training skill called "Pushing Hands." Broken down as follows:

*Single Push Hands:*
As it's name implies, it involves the placing of a single hand on a facing opponents wrist, who is required to deflect your incoming push to his/her head, heart and groin and immediately deflected, he /she returns the push to the same zones on your person, which you also deflect.

This develops the first four skills of the "Thirteen Postures" (see chapter ten): An = Push, Ghi = Press, Peng = Ward and Loy = Rollback.

*Double Push Hands:*
Again as it's name implies, it involves placing both hands on the forearm and wrist of your facing opponent, who busies himself/herself to not only deflect your push, but also to control you through the grasp and control skill known as; "Qin Na." This also concentrates on the first four but brings it into the realms of practical usage.

*Da Lu or Large Rollback Push Hands:*
Also known as Four Corners, it brings the drill to a much higher level, that helps develop the necessary skills of evasion and control. Utilising the imaginary four corners of a square, with the aid of nimble footwork, you draw your attacker into a corner with an arm breaking lock and pull technique. He/she is then forced to apply a break - out manoeuvre, that spins you around 270 degrees into the adjacent corner from which you also have break - out.

All eight arm skills of the Thirteen Postures are employed in this drill, the last four being: Lie = Split, Tsai = Pluck, Kao = Shoulder Stroke and Zhou = Elbow Stroke. In addition to the above, you introduce the last of the thirteen postures known as the five directions: Advance, Retreat, Step Left, Step Right and Hold the Centre also known as Central Equilibrium.

*Free Style Push Hands:*
When you have developed the footwork and hand skills of the above styles you enter the final level before you are exposed to full sparring. Free style is where you bring all your accumulated experience of push hands to bear. All thirteen postures are applied in a two person un choreographed battle of wits and skill which includes "Take Downs" for the first time.

In order to go deeper into Tai Chi and Qigong we must identify and examine their two most important ingredients namely; Yin and Yang or Tai Chi. Which is the name we call these two opposite forces when they are in full flow and working in harmony to create; "Balance." All postures of Tai Chi and Qigong for that matter, should contain their Yin and Yang elements. For example; all upward, outward and expanding movements are Yang, whilst sinking, inward and contracting movements are Yin. However, this is viewed from the martial perspective. When we are only considering the health aspects, then you should reverse the above, for example; outward now becomes Yin as this represents negative Qi release from the body, whereas inward is Yang, due to it's positive healthy Qi that's drawn into the body. Simplified it means fresh air in, stale air out.

Therefore Yin and Yang become uniquely relative to the situation viewed at the time. Compared to the sun which is classed as the most Yang thing in the universe, the earth is Yin. But, when compared to the moon the earth is Yang.

In motion the leg carrying the most weight is Yang, as is it's opposite arm/hand. The leg to be raised therefore becomes Yin, as does the opposite arm/hand likewise. When you come to rest and stand with the weight equally loaded into each foot, Yin and Yang forces of motion separate and return to an empty state the Chinese call; "Wu Chi" meaning Nothingness or Void.

A book I will be producing at a later date, will cover the Yin and Yang of the postures, both internally and externally in greater detail.

# CHAPTER FOUR

# FUNDAMENTAL BENEFITS

For the benefit of those of you who are new to Tai Chi I would like to briefly outline the fundamental benefits of regular practice.

## Posture.

I start with this as I believe it to be the most important principle of the form, when newcomers turn up at the class, I estimate maybe 90% show varying degrees of posture imbalance. This carries with it problems such as joint degeneration, due to unequal loading, in engineering terms this is known as; "Eccentric Loading". Brought about when the gravitational line in the body falls out of alignment. The first noticeable side effect being a restriction in the smooth function of the lungs, lowering the oxygen levels transported via the blood to the other organs.

A person with bad posture will accelerate wear and tear on the joints, due to this imposed distortion of the gravity line that is offset from the centre of the joints. The supporting muscles, tendons and ligaments which are likewise imbalanced and stressed, now strain to compensate for this excessive loading. Symptoms of which typically show up as Lumbago, Fibrositis and Sciatica etc... . Therefore the first step to bring the body back into correct alignment, is simply to start at the head by keeping it erect at all times placing it centrally above the torso.

## Coordination.

I am sure most newcomers to Tai Chi will agree with me that the majority of them have lost the coordination they enjoyed in their youth, often complaining of feeling clumsy and out of balance. An uncoordinated body will evidently lack in smooth Qi circulation, which manifests itself in the form of poor circulation of blood supply to the hands and feet. The reason for this is due to the body operating on "Localised" movement, which means; the arms for example moving in isolation from the rest of the body. The least exercised part of the body is the torso which happens to be the most important, as it houses the vital organs and spine. Which all rely on receiving a healthy supply of blood to the tissues, to function efficiently.

The problem is, people are generally not aware of the importance of keeping the torso both supple and erect, they move their arms, legs and neck throughout their day to day movements but fail to flex the spine or torso muscles anywhere near enough. Tai Chi uniquely brings all the joints and muscle groups into play in a coordinated manner. This eliminates the possibility of Qi stagnation, resulting in damaged tissues and an unhealthy build up of toxins, especially in the joints. The smooth rhythmic wave like motions of Tai Chi, operate to wash these toxins out and into the blood stream. Where they are expelled via the kidneys, thus eliminating the potential for conditions like Rheumatoid Arthritis to take hold.


**Regulating The Breath.**

When you combine poor posture and coordination you are restricting the lung function, this deficiency in posture creates a distortion to the natural shape of the torso, hindering the important function of the diaphragm. This in turn also stresses the other organs causing a distortion to their balance, which is communicated back to the lungs in the form of tightness leading to shortage of breath.

Add to this poor coordination, which as mentioned above results in localised stiffness to the joints, muscles and tendons and you will notice that it restricts the lungs even more. However, after many months of regular practice you will begin to sense your breathing down to your toes and fingertips. Meaning, the stiffness and tension that normally restricts the lungs full potential will have diminished. At this stage you become acutely aware of the therapeutic effect it is also having on the other organs, which materialises in the form of noticeable improvements in the body functions generally.

16

**Regulating The Mind.**

By grasping an appreciation of the philosophical aspects of Tai Chi, then putting them into practice, you are enveloping yourself with a protective shield to "external pressures" that so commonly cause us stress. Now recognised a major contributor to the poor health and premature deaths of countless thousands this century.

Yes stress is a killer and the more antidotes you have to it the better off you will be, in terms of quality of life and health generally. Regulating the breath, improving coordination and posture will have a positive effect on calming and focusing the mind. These are the fruits offered by Tai Chi and Qigong and through regular practice, you will discover all these things and more.

My Yang style Master Dr Yang Jwing Ming, talks of the mind being separated into two function areas; one is emotion and the other wisdom, both corresponding to Yin and Yang respectively. When emotions are prominent it means Yin is the controller, and it is here when the wisdom mind Yang, acts as the counterbalance to keep us on an even keel.

17

# CHAPTER FIVE

# TAI CHI AND QIGONG

# "FENG SHUI FOR LIFE"

In recent years, a great deal has been written on the concept of Feng shui, but what is maybe not understood or explained, is the inseparable link it has with Tai Chi and Qigong. In China history has recorded long periods of social unrest and conflict. However, the same can be said for it's opposite where peace and calm reigned supreme.

It was during these non warring years that many enlightened individuals spent their time in the practice of; "Spiritual and Physical Cultivation." These seeds grew into the deep philosophical and enlightened principles that were documented into the now well known and respected texts such as: the Nei Ching, Yi Ching and Tao Te Ching, all containing riches that spawned Tai Chi, Qigong and Feng Shui.

Feng Shui means; "Wind and Water," which in itself can be slightly misleading, as it actually represents all the elements that create life in the universe. It is a scientific belief system that encourages us to live in harmony with our surroundings. From the location and layout of our domestic dwellings to our place of work, where we spend most of our lives.

Those who drink the knowledge of Feng Shui will be guided to ensure at all times there is an abundance of healthy "Qi," which means "Life Force" or "Universal Energy." This energy is all embracing and flows through and touches everything that dwells within the universe.

When this natural flow is interrupted or distorted in any way, it creates negative Qi, effecting the health and prosperity of those it touches. The Qi therefore has become imbalanced which according to the Chinese means the Yin and Yang are not in harmony. These two forces representing both negative and positive energies respectively.

18

So, when Yin Qi balances equally with Yang Qi, they combine to create; "True or Healthy Qi" which can be seen in all healthy living matter. The Taoist Sages of old were said to be able to "see" the vibrations of this True Qi from the cultivation of their Taoist arts. This equilibrium between Yin and Yang in a global or universal sense is "Tai Chi," being the ultimate binding force that embraces and creates the "Ten Thousand Things," which was the Taoists way of saying literally, everything.

It seems to me therefore, that when we talk of Feng Shui we are describing the function and principles of Yin and Yang. Now the question is, how do we encapsulate this True or Healthy Qi? What is the secret that precipitates it's assimilation? The simple answer is, we need to create the "Bridges" or catalysts that link and convert the etheric to solid, these Bridges are in fact Tai Chi and Qigong.

Their practice encourages the mind and body to release the blockages that would otherwise act as a barrier to the creation and absorption of Qi. They open up senses that in most people lie dormant, but when stirred take the human species to new heights of sensitivity, awareness and health.

If Feng Shui therefore, depicts the environment in its positive or negative sense, then Tai Chi and Qigong enter the frame as champions of the cause by protecting us from the known and harmful affects of over exposure to extremes of Yin and Yang energies. Their role is to direct us into the "Middle Path," where positive healthy Qi exists.

Here are some examples of Feng Shui that appear all around us:

> In the garden there will be areas where most plants or shrubs refuse to prosper, (Yin Qi). Whilst only a few feet away they flourish, (Yang Qi).

> In Autumn, trees on one side of a road lose their leaves whilst the other side are still green and strong.

> In an open field of grass certain zones are deep green and lush whilst other zones look positively parched. A good example of this can be seen in a mushroom field, where they will only grow in the most fertile areas.

19

Villagers living on one side of a valley may record a higher
occurrence of arthritic and bronchial illness than those on
the other side.

Wild and domestic animals instinctively know where best
to site their sets, nests and dens etc... .

It is this "sense" that I believe lies dormant in man and distinguishes the
academic practitioner from Feng Shui Master. A true master not only
theoretically knows the pulse of this universal Qi but he/she can actually
see or feel it.

The Taoist arts which include Tai Chi, Qigong, Yoga and meditation
are the tools necessary in the development of this ability, that has for
centuries been suppressed by man's ignorance. But in this new age of
enlightenment even the "Die Hards" are finally opening their eyes to its
wonders.

# CHAPTER SIX

# CLASSICAL YANG QIGONG

The following Qigong (Fig's 1 to 17 inclusive), are designed to prepare the body through repetitive practice for Tai Chi, as they stimulate and flex all the joints, tendons, ligaments and muscles collectively described by the Chinese as; "Sinews." Which must be naturally relaxed in order for the Qi to circulate freely throughout the body. Each movement of the exercise must be in accord with the Classics (see chapter ten). That is to say, you must at all times keep the head erect, do not allow the torso to collapse, relax the shoulders, keep all four limbs supple not stiff and let the buttocks hang down naturally, free from any tension.

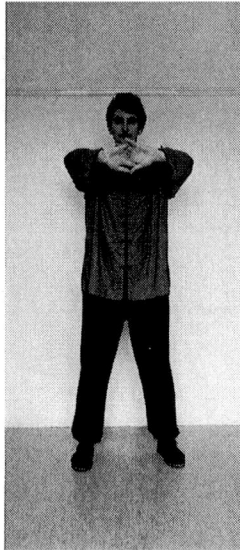

Fig. 1

Fig 2.

Fig 3

 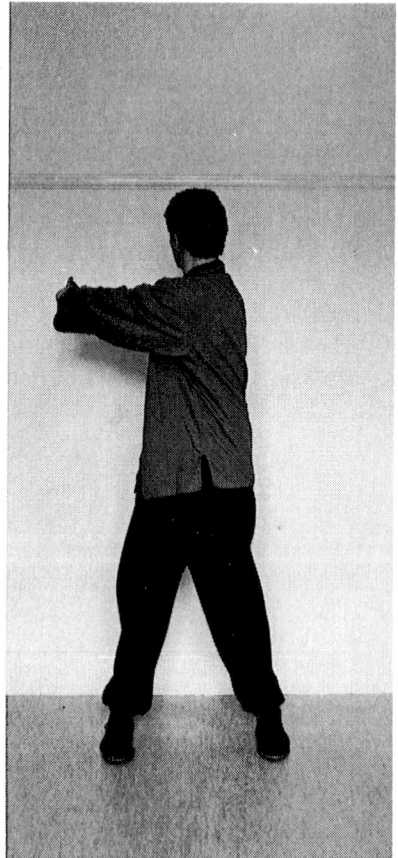

Figures 1-5: "Bending, Twisting, Stretching and Tilting."
This flexes, stretches and twists the spine releasing tension
and increasing flexibility. Relax all the joints and
muscles throughout.

Fig 4.

Fig 5.

Fig 6.          Fig 7.

Figures 6 and 7: "Advance and Retreat." Loosens the pelvic girdle to open up the waist for fluid movement, linking the Tai Chi postures for Yang (Advance) and Yin (Retreat).

Fig 8.  Fig 9.

Figures 8 and 9: "Open and Close the Chest." This helps link the spine to the arms and should be coordinated with smooth wave like movements through the torso.

**Fig 10.**  **Fig 11.**

Figures 10 - 15: "Tai Chi Figure 8." This develops flexibility
through the spine and helps you feel the Tai Chi symbol in a
three dimensional image, through it's spiral actions.

Fig 12.          Fig 13.

Fig 14.                              Fig 15.

Fig 16.                    F 17.

Figures 16 and 17: "Tai Chi Coordination." This involves all the joints of the body working in unison and is centred around pivoting the arms whilst alternate lifting of hands.

Fig 18.                    Fig 19.

Figures 18 - 23: "Six Hand Qigong." Postures to be performed whilst remaining perfectly still in; "Standing Qigong" which reshapes and rejuvenates the body.

30

Fig 20. Fig 21.

Fig 22.                    Fig 23.

**Six Hand Qigong.**

The preceding photographs (Fig's 18 to 23 inclusive) locates the hand positions of this special sequence of standing postures. Unfortunately still photographs are unable to capture the sublime interchange between each hand position. However, the most important thing is, correctly locating the finished and fixed postures shown in the illustrations.

In my opinion Six Hand Qigong is the fundamental foundation block of Tai Chi. Shown originally to me by Master Chu King Hung, it took me approximately ten years for me to fully appreciate it's hidden treasures, which I will now share with you by explaining it's; "Principle Benefits."

*Emptying:* The term; 'emptying' refers to releasing the body from tension both physically and mentally. To empty the mind you must train meditation skills which dissolves the negative thoughts, that in turn manifests into physical tension throughout the body. The standing postures of Six Hand Qigong, aligns the joints so that postural balance ensues. Facilitating the dissipation of tension zones such as the neck, shoulders and lower back.

*Rejuvenation:* This positive effect of postural balance allows the free flow of "Qi," to circulate around the body, thus nourishing the areas that previously received poor supply. Therefore all the sinews and organs are serviced as nature (Tao) intended and the net results are the rejuvenation of these tissues.

*Five Bows:* The "Five Bows" are two arms, two legs and the spine, all of which are responsible for the motorised movement of the body. A maxim often spouted by my teacher was; 'When the joints are locked the Qi is blocked.' What he basically meant, was you should keep the joints slightly curved to ensure fluidity of motion and Qi. Six Hand Qigong creates the necessary curves and in effect, "Switches On" the meridian circuit through the Bows, which should form the root of your body motion.

*Body Engineering:* The cumulative effects of Six hand Qigong realigns the skeletal structure to bring the force of gravity into the center of the joints. Thus creating structural stability and muscular balance which explains the term; "Rooting." Which is when you harness this incredibly powerful force to work with you as opposed to against you, when your posture is dysfunctional. The added benefit of having the gravitational line entering your head, travelling down unimpeded through the body and exiting the feet is, it reduces undue wear and tear on the joints.

*Qi Circulation:* The standing and sitting postures of Six Hand Qigong, coupled with regulating the breath develops both Small and Large Heavenly Cycles. Being the internal Qi circulation skills of advanced Tai Chi practice.

*Martial Qigong:* In addition to it's health promoting properties, it can also be categorised as Martial Qigong as it provides the necessary rooting, defensive and offensive angles used in self defence. And, it also helps develop the unique "Charging" of the muscle tissues associated with "Hard Style Qigong."

*Tai Chi Postures:* The curves and angles of Six Hand Qigong were primarily intended to provide the power shapes for your Tai Chi postures and therefore should form the inner core when practicing Tai Chi Form or Pushing Hands.

# CHAPTER SEVEN

# CLASSICAL YANG TAI CHI

This is a unique short form of Classical Yang Tai Chi Chuan, designed to give a beginner an easy ride into Tai Chi training. As I mentioned earlier, it is far less a burden to undertake a short form as your introduction to the art. All postures shown are Classical Yang and therefore will be useful for those students who are engaged in learning the Long Form, for reference purposes, regarding limb positions and the general spirit of the actions.

When you take up Tai Chi you will tend to practice it as Large or Big Frame, as all newcomers to the art stand quite high in their postures due to tension in the muscles, tendons and joints generally. You are also likely to overstretch the limbs, as initially you may find it hard to deeply relax and sink into your body, in the way you will notice more experienced practitioners do.

During the early stages you should constantly seek to relax all the joints, occasionally pausing to free any "Blockages" (areas of tension that disrupt your Qi from its smooth circulation), which is a goal of Tai Chi. Everyone without exception, will experience initial frustration when you realise your own levels of stiffness, poor coordination and the lack of mental focus in memorising the details of the postures.

You will at times feel you've got two left feet, spaghetti arms and a head that is on the wrong way round. However, this is when you must grit your teeth and carry on regardless, as those who fall at the first hurdle will always fail to complete the race. And in this case the race is for longevity and an opening up of the senses, which enhances and enriches the quality of your life.

Remember to breath in and out naturally through the nose only, whilst lightly keeping the tongue pressed up against the roof of the mouth. This will assist the regulation of the Qi around the torso, which is known as the "Small Heavenly Cycle," essential in keeping the body functions balanced.

35

Fig 24.                              Fig 25.

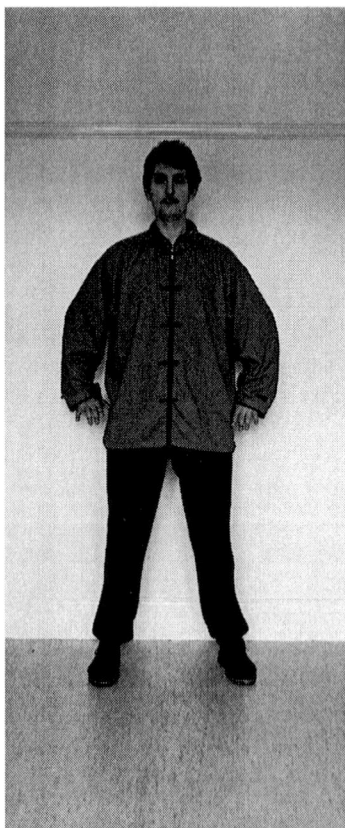
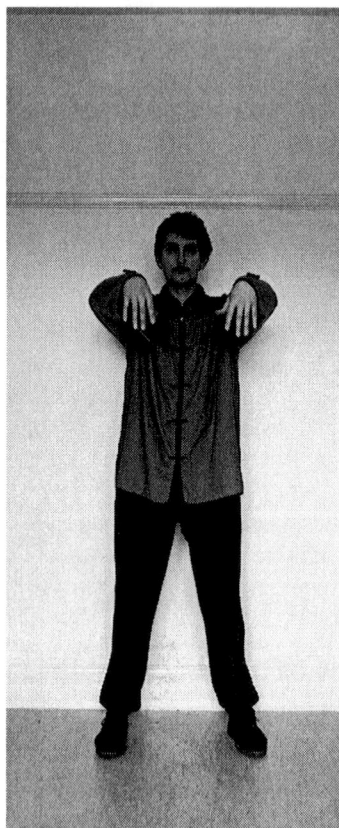

Figures 24 - 26: "Tai Chi Beginning" (Tai Chi Che Shih). Stand
perfectly erect and keep the head lifted throughout the whole
form as if it were suspended from above. (Facing north).

**Fig 26.**  **Fig 27.**

Figures 27 - 32: "Grasp The Bird`s Tail" (Lan Chiao Wei). This comprises four key postures known as Peng (Ward Off), Lu (Roll Back), Ghi (Press) and An (Push). (north on ward to left).

Fig 28.

Fig 29.

Figures 27 - 29: are Ward Off Left and Right with a 90 degree turn to the right between them (east). Remember push from the rear heel to square up the hips to face the front.

Fig 30.                    Fig 31.

Figure 30 is Roll Back and 31 is Press. When moving into Roll back turn the hips 45 degrees to the side, keep feet still and square up hips when applying Press (east).

Fig 32.                    Fig 33.

Figure 32 is Push. Figures 33 - 35: "Single Whip" (Tan Pien).
Comprising three movements: Look Left, Look Right and the
"Whip." Fig 33 is Look Left (north west).

Fig 34.                Fig 35.

Figure 34 is Look Right which is a 90 degree turn of the hips. Feet to remain fixed (north east). Fig 35 is the Whip keep the rear arm straight but not locked (west).

Fig 36.                    Fig 37.

Figures 36 - 37: "Lifting Hands Step Up" (Ti Shou Shang Shih).
Comprising two movements: Fig 36 Lift Hands and Fig 37 Step
Up. Step up is also known as Elbow Stroke. (north).

Fig 38.  Fig 39.

Figure 38: "White Crane Airs Wings" (Pai Hao Liang Chih).
Fig 39: "Brush Knee and Twist Step". (Tso Lou Hsih Au Pu)
Feel the "Balance Point" that links the two. (west).

Fig 40.　　　　　　　　　　　　　Fig 39 Rpt.

Figure 40: "Play The Pi Pa" (Shou Hui Pi Pa). From the preceding posture flow into this as both arms form two spiral clockwise patterns. Repeat Fig 39. (still west).

Fig 41.                    Fig 39 Rpt.

Figure 41: "As 39 But Left Hand." In the twist step ensure the knee of the supporting leg projects just beyond the toes, as this aids stability whilst stepping. (west).

45

Figures 42 - 43: "Deflect Down Parry and Punch". (Chin Pu
Pan Lan Chui). From previous posture circle right fist and
Parry with left hand (Fig 42) Step and Punch (Fig 43) (west).

Fig 44.          Fig 45.

Figures 44 -45: "As If Shut Up" (Yu Feng Shih Pi). Also
known as Withdraw and Push, the left hand slides under
the right arm which withdraws and pushes. (west).

**Fig 46**                    **Fig 41 Rpt.**

Figures 46 -41Rpt "Embrace Tiger and Return To Mountain"
(Pao Hu Kuei Shan). Turn 90 degrees to the right and step
into fig 46. Pivot to rear on left foot into fig 41. (sth east).

Fig 47.                    Fig 48.

Figure 47: "Seeing Fist Under Elbow" (Chou Ti Kan Chui) and
Fig 48: "Backstepping Monkey" (Tso Tao Nien Hou). Repeat
Figs 30 - 33 after Fig 41 turning into Fig 47 (west). Step back
three times landing in Fig 48. (west). When stepping back
the knees to stay bent keeping the head parallel to the floor.

Figure 49: "Diagonal Flight" (Hsieh Fei Shih) and Fig 50: "Wave Hands Like Clouds"(Yuen Shou).  From Fig 48 turn 90 degrees to right into Fig 49 (north), then flow straight into Fig 50 and step three times to the left (still facing north).

Figure 51: "Lower The Snake Body" (Shih Shen Hsia Shih) and
Fig 52: "Golden Cock Stands On One Leg" (Chin Chi Tu Li).
Repeat Figs 30, 34 and 35 turning 90 degrees (west) then drop
down into Fig 51. Sweep up into Fig 52 then take one step
back to create a mirror image ie: left hand and leg raised. (west).

Fig 53.                                    Fig 54.

Figure 53: "Stand High To Examine The Horse" (Kan T`an Ma).
Fig 54 "Separate Right Foot" (Yu Fen Chiao). From Fig 52 sink
down on the same leg into Fig 53 and then step 45 degrees to
the left into fig 54. (sth west). Direct kick to the north west.

Fig 55.                    Fig 56.

Figure 55: "Turn and Kick With Heel" (Chuan Shen Teng
Chiao) and Fig 56: "Step Up and Punch Down" (Chin Pu
Tsai Ch'ui). After Fig 54:" Separate Foot" with left foot turn
into Fig 55, rpt Figs 39 and 41, finish up in Fig 56 (east).

**Fig 57.**                         **Fig 58.**

Figures 57 - 59: "Fair Lady Weaves Shuttle" (Yu Nu Ch`uan Suo). After Fig 58 completely rpt Figs 28 - 32 (east). Then add Figs 33 - 35 (west). Turn 180 degrees into Fig 57 onto Fig 58 (east) and step 45 degrees into Fig 59 (north east).

Fig 59.                    Fig 60.

Figure 60: "Step Forward To Seven Stars" (Shang Pu Ch`i Hsing). After Fig 59 complete Three other points on the compass (4 Corners) then add Figs 28 - 35 plus Fig 51 and sweep up into Fig 60 (west). * Note - the other directions of the 3 remaining corners are: Nth Wst, Sth Wst, Sth Est.

Fig 61.                           Fig 62

Figure 61: "Step Back and Ride the Tiger" (T'ui Pu K'ua Fu)
Fig 62: "Turn Body and Sweep Lotus with Leg" (Chuan Shen
Pai Lien). From Fig 60 step back facing same direction into
Fig 61 then turn 360 degrees into Fig 62 (west).

Fig 63.                              Fig 64.

Figure 63: "Draw the Bow and Shoot the Tiger" (Wan Kung She Fu). Fig 64: " Close Tai Chi" ( Ho Tai Chi). From Fig 62 slap hands onto right leg/foot and land in Fig 63 (north west). Rpt Figs 42 - 46 except hands cross lower down as Fig 64. To complete form reverse Figs 24 - 25 from Fig 64 (north).

# CHAPTER EIGHT

# EXPERIENCES

This chapter will deal my observations on the state of the nations health and I won't be pulling punches. I also intend to enlighten you to the physical and emotional changes that takes place during your practice years. Covering the period from day one, through to ten years with the aid of a paper I wrote many years ago called; "The Five Gates Of Tai Chi." As an example I will share with you my own "Experiences" and those of others whom I've encountered along the way, as a teacher and student.

**Tai Chi And Qigong - The Attraction.**

First ask yourself why are you attracted to these arts? And let's see how you compare to me. By 1979 I was not exactly in the best of health for my age, after years working as an apprentice plumber forced to kneel on concrete floors with no protective knee pads because; 'that's for wimps only.' So, consequently by the end of the nineteen seventies I was diagnosed with have early signs of Rheumatism in my knees and hips.

As if that wasn't enough, I also had to deal with a weakness to the left side of my body caused by an adverse reaction to the Polio vaccine when I was a young child. Up to the point when Tai Chi entered my life I still as an adult, suffered from a "Clicky" left hip and a weakened left lung. All resulting from the Polio flare up and not to mention the many subsequent chest infections I contracted every time I caught a cold or especially the flu.

Physically I was also plagued by a damaged shoulder blade (Scapula) and surrounding tissue. Caused from a foolish incident when I got into a fight in my late teens with a club bouncer, who in all fairness did his job very efficiently, by bouncing me down a flight of concrete steps on my back. The fact that I didn't seek professional treatment for the shoulder contributed to the many years of ensuing pain I suffered. At least half a dozen times a year it would go into spasm, consistently reminding me of my stupidity. And as if the above wasn't enough, I also regularly suffered from indigestion, migraine and poor circulation to my limbs especially legs that would often cramp up in my sleep, giving me a rude awakening. The above no doubt assisted by the high stress levels prevalent in my life at the time which I had no idea how to deal with.

All in all I wasn't a healthy specimen. But, that began to change when I reached the safe haven of Tai Chi and Qigong. From the moment I started I knew it was special, within a few months I was feeling much more relaxed. Though I was clearly well below the "Average Base Line," which meant it would take me a while just to get back up to average health. I estimate I reached the line after two years, which isn't that bad considering the deprived state I was originally in.

The goal thereafter is to steadily progress upward above the line, which I'm pleased to say I have and continue to do. The catalogue of ailments pre - Tai Chi are I'm pleased to say no longer with me. Nowadays, although middle aged, instead of experiencing the degeneration of ageing, I appear to be getting stronger physically and emotionally as years roll on.

**Student Stories.**

Now let's look at the experiences of those dedicated students whom persevere and achieve the expected results:-

A elderly lady who has only been to my class a few times recently approached me and showed me her hands and commented; 'You know I'm really chuffed how Tai Chi takes the swelling away.' She was talking of the painful swelling to her finger joints and especially the knuckles caused by Rheumatoid Arthritis.

A lovely lady called Bronwyn turned up at my class with what I can only describe as an; "advanced stress racked body." And to be honest she was possibly the most uptight person I think I've ever met. This showed itself in her posture and physique which I recently reminded her was like a dried out brittle twig. Generally her health was poor because of this stiffness. However, I'm pleased to report she has released her body from it's destructive grip, looking and feeling 100% healthier.

Nearly three years ago a young lady called Debbie appeared at my class with her mother and sister. She was recovering from open heart surgery and had adopted a posture that was very Yin ie: concaved chest rounded upper back. This created and encouraged the blocking of Qi in the Yang rising channel of the spine (Du) and the balancing Yin channel to the front of the torso (Ren). The effects of this were clearly visible by the sallow pallor of her face and the white cold touch of her hands. So cold were they she would have to wear gloves despite the room being reasonably warm. Gradually things improved to the point she not only doesn't have to adorn the gloves anymore, but she now assists me in teaching the art. And how did she achieve this? Hard work, nothing less would do for her and as a result she sings the praises of Tai Chi louder than anyone I know.


**Happy Qi.**

If you attend one of my classes you would know why I couldn't produce a book without some form of humour embedded amongst its pages. After all it was Master Chu who said; 'Encourage laughter in your class as it creates "Happy Qi," raising everyone's spirits which in turn nourishes the immune system.' In this section I will poke a little gentle fun at my own students and some of the unusual types I've encountered along the way. See if you recognise yourself in the types of person I now list below:-

*The: "Honey Bee."*
The honey Bee is a warm and endearing type of person, that unfortunately is unable through genetic programming to attend the class for more than one or two sessions without flitting off to try something else to pollinate.

*The: 'Oh... I've Been Looking For Tai Chi For Ages.'*
These are unfortunately very common, they often bother the hell out of me with their sincere phone calls. Instantly recognisable they bleat on and on and on about their problems and swear blind they'll be at the next class session. They NEVER turn up.

*The: 'I know I'm Talented.'*
Not so common, they appear at the class and pick up the skills very quickly. Others feel almost inadequate in their presence. After usually half a dozen sessions they peak and leave, having satisfied some perverse instinct that drains their enthusiasm the moment they realise they can do it.

*The: 'I Can't Do That, Can I ?'*
This type tip toes into the class and do their best to blend in with the wall covering. When I eventually spot them their eyes betray their total lack of self confidence. I have to constantly reassure them that they are progressing otherwise they go. But, the most amusing thing is, when they are obviously doing something right they still insist they can't do it.

*The: "Stormers."*
These are thankfully few in number, but do exist. They only appear for one lesson or should I say half a lesson. The void where their brains should be, is filled with Nitro-Glycerine, just waiting to "Go Off." For some strange reason they are unable to accept constructive criticism without blowing up and storming off. For example: I noticed a lady who had just joined the class was forcing her knees back against the joints, so I simply explained how it was blocking her Qi in the legs. Her reaction shocked the class when she raged; 'Right, that's it.... I'm off! I'm not putting up with this!' And off she stormed leaving us all perplexed.

*The: "Psychic Vampires."*
These are by no means sinister in their intentions, its just that they don't know their doing it. A Psychic Vampire is a person who has lost the ability to blink. Their eyes are permanently fixed on their intended target (usually me or some other Tai Chi teacher) whom they transfix with their dark penetrating gaze like a rabbit caught in headlights. Whilst your trapped in their incessant energy sapping grip, you try to break their glare by feverishly cracking jokes to make them laugh. Unfortunately Psychic Vampires have also lost their sense of humour, for whilst all others around them are falling about laughing they remain poker faced and still locked onto your now nervously twitching face. Their arrival at the class is usually heralded by the spooky way the door opens by itself and the rolling mist that pours into the room through the doorway. Immediately

following a sudden temperature drop, they appear being carried along on the misty carpet with no visible signs of leg movement.

At a holiday centre I regularly teach at, I was telling the new batch of students about a "PV" that had graced me with her presence the previous week. When I noticed another one sat on a bench a short distance away on her own. After observing her for approximately fifteen minutes I announced; 'Don't look now but there's one over there.' After everyone had less than subtly located her transfixed peering face, a man's voice shot out from the crowd; 'That's no vampire! that's my wife!' My embarrassment was so distressing I decided the best course of action would be to disappear up my own back passage. Which I did to resounding applause.

### The: 'Ooops... I've Popped.'
Becoming more common nowadays, these take me too literally when I say, 'Sink the Qi.' Probably as a result of some congenital defect they invade our classes with their uncontrollable flatulence, fired into action during either a bending or a deep squatting exercise. The result of their actions can be seen etched on the red faces of the students in their immediate vicinity. More often than not however, they remain unmoved and carry on as if it never happened.

### The: 'My Brain Has Left My Skull.'
With the odd exception these types are usually let's say; "getting on in years." Fairly common, they are instantly recognisable by the far away look in their eyes, that descends on them the moment I require them to perform a Qigong or Tai Chi manoeuvre. Another more fundamental way of identifying them is by their brain, which by some strange phenomenon has miraculously appeared on the outside of the skull. Detaching itself from the rest of the body.

The result of this leaves them flapping, if required to complete the most simple of movements such as raise the right foot. Because the brain is now further away than it should be, the signal takes much longer to reach it. Frustration now creeps in whilst their waiting for the reply, so in order to not be left behind they raise their left hand instead. This strange affliction happily becomes rectified after approximately six months when the brain is seen to return to its rightful place as chief body coordinator.

*The: 'I Get High On Qi.'*
These are generally latter day Hippies or Hippy revivalists, who find Tai Chi is on the same; "Cosmic Wavelength" as they are. The perpetual serene look etched on their faces positively glows when they experience their first "Rush of Qi." Which they swear brings them closer to; "Nirvana." You would not find it too difficult to spot one as they tend to stand out with their bare feet, pony tails and catweazle like whispy beards, and the men are just the same.

*The: 'Instant Instructors.'*
Quite common though as an instructor I welcome their help most of the time. This type of person is born with a natural instinct to innocently and credibly teach everyone they come into contact with. A good but fairly extreme example would be the character create by Harry Enfield whose catch phrase is; 'You don't want to do it like that, you should do it like this!' It is not uncommon in my experience for them to start teaching in the class during their very first session. Usually preying on the, 'My Brain Has Left My Skull' types, by showing them a different way to incorrectly do what they were already doing incorrectly.

*The: 'Holiday Makers.'*
I'd like to take this opportunity to say "hello everyone," as these tend to be the majority shareholders in the classes around the UK. In the main they're ladies who come week in week out with their friend or friends for their regular fix of "Keep Fit Tai Chi." Whilst interested in the "Internal" aspects and the variety of exercise patterns, they obviously don't carry their training to the home as I always insist they should. They do progress but plainly much slower than the "Staunchers" whom they're often seen watching with admiration. However no criticism is placed their way because they provide necessary light hearted humour, chit-chat, and gossip that I encourage in my classes to create "Happy Qi." Also, although uncommon, in the past some of my "Staunchers" have been recruited from the ranks of the "Holidaymakers."

*The: 'Staunchers.'*
These are my senior students, of varying personalities that all have one thing in common; "Dedication." Their attendance rates are very high, they train at home and in some cases in work (when the bosses aren't

watching). Any Tai Chi teacher will tell you they are the backbone and support network of the school, without whom it is impossible to develop as a teacher or bring the skills to a wider audience.

*The: 'Bungie Jumper.'*
The only way to identify these is the way they burst through the classroom (Kwoon) doors on the end of a giant length of Bungie cord. And, at the close of the session the cord suddenly becomes taught again and yanks them back out. Now this cord must be incredibly long for it can take usually two to three weeks for it to spring them back in through the doors again. Once returned they stand in exactly the same territorial spot chosen previously and act as if they've never been away,

**Five Gates Of Tai Chi.**

As you begin your Tai Chi practice for the first time you ask yourself, 'what will it do for me?' To answer this I will now describe what the average person can expect as you journey through the; "Five Gates of Tai Chi."

Gate One - First Month:- *Self Realisation.* You will become aware of your tension and stress levels, stiffness in joints and limbs, the lack of balance and coordination, poor quality of your breathing, general irregularities in your posture and lack of Qi circulation. Note! At this stage your emotions display frustration when you realise you own limitations.

Gate Two - After Six Months:- *Basic Changes.* Your tension and stress levels begin to drop, joints and limbs become more fluid, balance and coordination improves, breathing function begins to sink, stiff and tense muscles relax, posture improves and an awareness of your own Qi develops. Note! Tai Chi pays huge dividends to those who try hard, those whom lack in effort will lack in reward.

Gate Three - After Two Years:- *Inner Awareness.* Qi begins its journey to the extremities of your limbs. The beneficial changes to your posture free the breath, balance and coordination become refined, the Yi and Shen

(Mind and Spirit) are stirred, joints and limbs generally loosen. There are also noticeable changes to skin tone and condition and Qi gathers at the Dan Tien ( Energy Centre). Note! Having experienced the above beneficial changes, your appetite grows and you hunger for further development.

Gate Four - After Five Years:- *Point of No Return.* The breath (Qi) propels all the limbs, the spirit unites with the Dan Tien and other associated Qi pathways. Stress becomes bridled and it's symptoms dissipate as you become physically and emotionally stronger. Less sleep is needed, common ailments such as colds and flu pass you by, your actions become instinctive, eyesight becomes clearer, eyes become clearer and your height marginally increases due to posture improvements. Yin and Yang energies flow without restriction and thus harmonise, hearing becomes sharper and all joints of the body are made buoyant by Qi. Note! Continuation beyond this gate will expose you to the true Taoist experience.

Gate Five - After Ten Years:- *The Journey Begins.* Human frailty is no longer of concern, the powers of mother nature (Tao) are seen for the first time, sixth sense develops through the opening of the upper Dan Tien, healing powers appear and Ching (Sexual Energy) is absorbed through regulating this activity. The Dan Tien becomes the centre of the universe and others feel your presence. Note! Beyond this gate lies the universe where all barriers dissolve and the Shen is free to dwell amongst the cosmos.

**State Of The Nation.**

A great frustration of mine is having accumulated this divine knowledge, is that I have become acutely aware of the general misconception of the nation who still believe being fit is healthy. Just ask one of the many middle aged fitness fanatics in these large health and fitness centres springing up all over the country, whom I've personally seen wheeled out on a paramedics stretcher on route to the local hospital; 'are you healthy?' and I'm sure they would answer; 'I thought I was.' As a professional full time Tai Chi teacher I come into contact with what I believe on a weekly basis is a typical cross-section of the population from children through to the elderly.  And the surprising thing is considering this is the new millennium, the younger generation are sadly lacking regular healthy exercise.  The age of the computer is having a detrimental affect by distracting them from seeking enjoyment outdoors with friends, as was the case with my own generation.

Besides my own, I would suggest all earlier generations were much closer to nature and were far more physically active in their pastimes.  However, as adults we let ourselves down, mainly due to lack of guidance from our elders in how to look after our health.  For example: smoking was almost actively encouraged by the government at the time, who did us no favours by being regularly seen smoking in public, no doubt much to the pleasure of the tobacco industry.  Although health and fitness studios were few and far between in those days, the children were definitely fitter and healthier than today.  But, as I said, that's not necessarily the case for adults.

Young adults today at least have the benefit of knowledge made readily available through the press and  media, that clearly spells out the hazards of over indulgence of alcohol, smoking and drug abuse.  Though a surprising number still choose to bury their heads in the sand, but will as they say; "pay the penalty" in later life.  As recently reported by the department of health, on the disturbing increase of lung cancer in young women who seem to be the worst culprits in ignoring the cigarette health warnings.

The "Smoky Generations," as I call them have over the last century kept the health service gainfully employed with conditions that in the main could have been avoided.  The mentality present in those days however, didn't offer much support to a healthier life-style.  An example of this blatant ignorance can be seen from my own experience as a tradesman in the construction industry where; "We were hard."  Protective clothing? pah..., dust masks?, ear plugs?, safety helmets?, washing of hands after handling chemicals and lead pipes?.......'Only  nance-bags do that.'

To put the total lack of regard for our health and wellbeing into perspective, I'll relate an experience I had in the late seventies when I worked as a pipefitter stripping out and repairing chemical carrying pipework during the shut down period in a large textiles factory.  On one occasion I spent a day in an area of the factory that was so toxic, by the end of the shift, the coins and my car keys had changed colour whilst in my jeans pocket. God only knows what damage that did to the poor souls who worked in there on a daily basis, when the factory was in full production.

Nowadays, things have improved but the legacy of this blatant ignorance lives on through the many sufferers of industrial related diseases. Their plight kept quiet by an embarrassed government and industry that conveniently chooses to brush it away under the carpet from public view. Just ask your area health authority how many people are presently being treated in this category and I think you will be surprised.

However, that is the past from which I hope we have and still are learning the painful lessons of our apathy as a nation. The future must now be driven by an enlightened government to take the message to the schools that; "Healthy is Cool."

# CHAPTER NINE

# TAOIST MEDITATION

Taoist meditation is an integral part of Tai Chi and Qigong training, it is the method of regulating breathing and therefore the Qi throughout the meridian system of the body. I also use meditation as a method of escapism from the pressure of the "External." These pressures can be looked on as loud and oppressive, therefore to counter, you must retreat into the self to seek peace and serenity. Historically Taoist Meditation runs hand in hand with Qigong, in that it was well established before Tai Chi reared it's head. It is the means by which the Taoist Sages of old achieved their ultimate goal; "Enlightenment."

In the practice of Tai Chi or Qigong it is important to develop the "Internal," categorised as Yin, to mutually flow and harmonise with the "External," Yang. Meditation is the vital ingredient to achieve this harmony and therefore should be practised with the same regularity as physical external patterns of exercise.

Whilst it is widely acknowledged in Tai Chi circles that there are three method of meditation practice, personally I only recommend two, namely: standing and sitting. The third is lying down, but the problem with this method is two fold. One, it is too easy to step over the fine line that exists between meditation and sleep. And two, if the goal is to create strong Qi circulation especially in the Ren and Du meridians then lying down is hardly conducive to this.

Before we go into the actual details of practicing meditation, I think it wise to distinguish between the popular Buddhist way and the Taoist method that I am covering here. Both are designed to achieve the same result ie; "Personal Self Enlightenment." As you see I describe it as something personal, that which cannot be shared with others, therefore to propose my experiences whilst meditating are the norm for all, would be misleading. As far as I am aware, the only difference between Buddhist and Taoist methods are the breathing patterns. Taoist start with natural breathing ie: abdomen rises as you breathe in, then reverses the process which is the pure "Taoist" method. Finally returning back to the natural rhythm to finish the session. Buddhist however base all the process on the natural pattern and because of the uniqueness I mentioned above, nobody could truly state which is the better method. Both are proven and tried over many centuries, therefore it must eventually come down to personal preference, which I leave to you.

**Standing Meditation.**

In standing meditation the Chinese say; 'You must stand tall and be rooted to the ground like a tree.' The legs can be straight (NB, the knees should not be pushed back against the joints, but left relaxed central for correct alignment), or bent in a squatting stance as in the standard Horse Stance seen in fig's 18 to 23. Standing still whilst holding a Tai Chi posture is also practiced to develop Yang Qi in a Yang posture (see fig 27) or Yin Qi in a Yin posture (see fig 61). A good example of standing meditation is Six Hand Qigong which I covered earlier. Whilst both sitting and standing styles are to be practiced in parallel, standing is regarded as slightly more advanced as it develops; "Grand Circulation" ie: Qi freely flowing throughout the whole body as opposed to; "Small" that remains in the torso, which in the stages of development must be established before the "Grand" is possible.

**Sitting Meditation.**

In sitting meditation as with standing, the arms can move or remain still. When moving the arms you are training the Qi to circulate up and down both torso and arms respectively. However, whilst sitting with no arm movements the Qi is focused into the torso and head only. This is known as; "Centring." As the name implies you are to sit down and make yourself as comfortable as possible, on a straight backed chair with the feet hip width apart, toes forward and parallel to each other. Or alternatively you could sit on the floor on a cushion, to raise the buttocks higher than the feet for good lumbar alignment. In this method the legs should be crossed or folded to concentrate the Qi into the torso and head only. Sitting is the preferred way to develop the "Small Heavenly Cycle," which entails opening up the two major channels of the torso and head known as the "Du." Yang by nature, it runs from a point between the legs known as; the "Hui Yin," to the head up the spine, and the "Ren" Yin by nature, that forms the other half of the circuit, running from the head down the front of the body to rejoin the Hui Yin. By creating a strong flow throughout this circuit, all Yin and Yang organs are said to received a healthy supply of Qi and the immune system becomes very robust.

Beyond the two goals mentioned above lies the cultivation of; the "Shen" or "Spirit." Which I hope to cover in more detail in a future "Intermediate and Advanced" Tai Chi book. However, in the meantime let us concentrate on the; "Do's and Don'ts" for good meditation practice:-

Practice daily but not in excess, 10 minutes per session is adequate for beginners.

Leave at least one hour to elapse after a large meal before meditating.

Do not meditate whilst under the influence of drugs or alcohol

Warm up the body to regulate the Qi before commencing.

Showering or bathing before-hand will help relax the body and mind to assist the circulation of Qi.

Never meditate whilst you are exhausted or emotionally charged.

Use your natural instincts to locate the best place to practice inside or outside the home.

If outdoors do not meditate in extremes of climate eg: windy, rainy, humid, hot, cold, damp conditions or direct summer sunlight.

After completion of the session gently massage the body.

**Typical Meditation Session.**

Assuming you have adhered to the advice given above, I will now take you through the basic process of actual Taoist Sitting Meditation:-

Rest the eyelids, do not completely shut them.

Lift the head to straighten up the torso and neck to free the diaphragm.

Place your tongue on the roof of your mouth with its tip touching behind the two upper front teeth, to form the connecting bridge for the Du and the Ren channels.

Breathe in and out through the nose training the breath to gently sink down and inflate the abdomen.

Place both hands with palms facing in over the Qi Hai point located directly below the navel. NB: Ladies, left hand over right and gents right over left.

Gently sink the breath down to where your hands are now placed, creating a sense of expansion and contraction throughout the whole pelvic basin.

Empty your mind of any distracting thoughts, leaving only the soft cyclic sounds of your breathing in your consciousness.

Keep your upper and lower teeth lightly touching, and swallow any saliva that accumulates linking it to an outward breath.

Allow yourself to drift to a special place where you arrived half way between asleep and awake. This is the location of your inner peace, that once discovered can be returned to, to refresh body mind and spirit.

# CHAPTER TEN

# TAI CHI CLASSICS
# &
# THE THIRTEEN POSTURES

Throughout this book though I occasionally make reference to the "Classics," there won't be a page that they don't touch in one way or another. They are the very core of correct practice and application of the art. Therefore no book on Tai Chi could be written without mentioning the fundamentally important "Classics" and "13 Postures."

In a nutshell the Classics are the ancient maxims that describe how to practice Tai Chi correctly. Whereas the 13 Postures are the specific posture shapes, directions and principles for physically practicing the art.

## THE CLASSICS.

These are attributed to Chang San Feng whose contribution to the creation of Tai Chi I have covered in chapter three. However, in support of his embryonic art he is reputed to have written an "Instruction Manual." Containing it's inner secrets that have since been handed down from master to disciple over the ensuing centuries, evolving into what we now call the "Classics."

Though there were more, they have been condensed into a total of Ten Key Maxims split equally into five external and five internal. "The External Classics" categorised as Yang, start at the head and gradually work their way down to the feet, ending with the description of the process that unifies them all.

Whilst the "Internal Classics" cover all that is needed to; "Internalise" your Tai Chi, categorised as Yin.

**External Classics.**

1. *Suspend The Head From Above:* The first thing to establish is what they mean by this. To raise the head you must locate an important energy cavity known as the; "Bai Hui," that resides at the crown of the head. By lifting this point everything below straightens out and as a result it is effectively the leading principle for posture correction.

By gently lifting and centring the head, the body noticeably becomes more light and agile, this in turn aids the breathing due to immediate structural improvement to the skeletal frame. Also, without the head being raised in this position you would find it difficult to establish the Shen in its proper place, behind the Sky Eye or Third Eye on the forehead.

2. *Sink The Shoulders and The Elbows:* This is quite simple; in that if you do as it says the Qi sinks to the Dan Tien and feet to establish your root. If your shoulders are raised, commonly seen in those who harbour tension in their bodies, the Qi becomes stagnated, trapped in the chest and upper back. Which restricts the smooth circulation of the Qi throughout the Ren and Du channels of the torso leaving one feeling out of sorts and out of balance. From a martial point of view, sinking the shoulders and elbows strengthens your posture to face a powerful incoming force, to the point a much smaller person can repulse a bigger and heavier aggressor by a combination of rooting and body positioning.

3. *Hollow The Chest and Raise The Upper Back:* This is a classic example of where we westerners misunderstood the Classics. Like anything that is new and exciting and has earnings potential, it will attract the attention of; "Bandwagon Jumpers." With either no or very little experience they read the Classics at face value and as a result they stood out a mile from the those students who had received proper training from a recognised Chinese master. In the early nineteen eighties I christened them the, "Hunchbacks," as they believed to practice the art correctly you must do exactly as this Classic says; "Hollow the chest and raise the upper back." What they didn't realise is that you should not remain fixed in this position, instead you should flow in and out of it depending on where you are in the specific posture. Nowadays good traditional Tai Chi teachers have established themselves in most regions of the country and therefore

thankfully this problem no longer exists. Now having got that off my chest I'll explain the purpose of the Classic: By hollowing the chest you form a "Bow" in the spine which encourages the Qi (For Health) or Jing (For Martial Power) to rise up to the shoulders and middle upper back, a point known as; the "Jai Ji" or root of the arms. At this stage we call this potential power posture "Peng" which means; "To Ward Off." or "Bounce Off."

By remaining fixed in this position the Qi or Jing simply won't budge, it just sits there and within a short period of time if not released, causes blockage to the system. Therefore like the string of a bow drawn to fire an arrow, you must release the spine to discharge it's stored energy. By allowing it to spring forward slowly for health or fast for martial, whereupon the upper torso returns to its rightful upright not bowed position. This is how you send the Qi or Jing down the arms for healthy limb circulation or Jing power explosion through the elbows, forearms or hands. Finally, the wave this creates in the torso aids the lung function generally.

**4.** *Loosen The Waist and Droop The Buttocks:* Firstly, by loosening the waist you open up and improve the Qi = Oxygenated Blood circulation throughout the whole pelvic basin. And by drooping the buttocks, the girdle releases the lower back and positions the pelvic basin to gravitationally align all localised organs, ie: Small Intestine, Large Intestine and Bladder. The reproductive organs and glands also receive nourishment through the combined effect of these two principles.

In order to create this freedom of movement you must spend time opening and thus lubricating the "Hips." The point where the hips connect to the pelvis is called; the "Qua," loosely translated it means; the "Crease Line," that is the folding and joining point between the upper thigh and the groin. When the Qua is open, Qi can freely circulate into the legs and hip joints thus eliminating the damaging toxins.

When you have released the hips, waist and lower back you must then train the girdle itself to become the "Director Of Operations." Ensuring all future movements are coordinated and directed through the waist generally. Emanating from the now newly discovered central core position of the body known as; "The Real Dan Tien." But beware, just as the mistake made in the Third Classic, don't read it at face value. Though the buttocks are to naturally hang down loosely, they should also gently

74

flex back and forth when the body is in motion. Or in other words, don't jam it into a lowered position then hold it there, otherwise it will lose it's shock absorbing function and ultimately damage the joints your trying to protect.

5. *All Movements Should Start In The Feet And Materialise In The Hands:* The fifth External Classic is designed to unite all the previous four (see coordination section In chapter four). Having now established your root, a downward push into the ground through the feet will create an upward resultant force, that if harnessed and directed centrally through the joints, tendons and muscles, forms this unique to Tai Chi; "Body Wave." However, this is still at this stage classed as External until you add the mind and the breath which Internalises the whole process. Leading us neatly to the next series of "Internal Classics."

**Internal Classics.**

6. *Unify The Internal With The External:* This is the unification of external physical movement with the natural rhythmic processes of the internal. And at its core lies the breath, which through training must be made to achieve its full potential. When we link this improved breathing function to the now correctly aligned and coordinated physical body, the Yin and Yang become balanced and total harmony ensues. But, remember, to ensure you create smooth Qi circulation you must match the external to the natural internal ebb and flow of the breath. Which in turn dictates the pace or frequency of your outer physical movements. The only time your internal is in a way led by the external is during combat training or the real thing, where you employ a special martial breathing skill known as; "Heng and Ha." Though this method still should coordinate the internal with the external, it should in no way be confused with the health promoting slow natural movements that have become the trade mark of Tai Chi.

7. *Distinguish Between Substantial and Insubstantial:* Before you commence your Tai Chi sequence you should stand with feet together and hands by your sides, head upright and close the eyes. The breathing should be long and made to sink to the abdomen and there you should

remain in a state the Chinese call; "Wu Chi" or nothingness. It is from this void it is believed all things originate in the universe including Yin and Yang. Having reached this peaceful and empty condition, the moment you step out to begin your Tai Chi form irrespective of style chosen, Yin and Yang separate and appear. Now the secret is, to bring the two together in a mutual cyclic balanced action through the external and internal processes of Tai Chi. In order to help these immensely powerful yet opposing forces to join in a form of "Cosmic Dance," you must learn the Yin and Yang of the Tai Chi postures externally and internally respectively.

All movements forward and upward are Yang by nature, therefore backwards and downwards must be Yin. And within these movements irrespective of direction there lies further Yin and Yang divisions, eg: the leg carrying most of the body weight is deemed substantial and therefore Yang. Whilst the other less or non load bearing leg is insubstantial and Yin. The arm/hand on the opposite side of the body to the substantial leg is correspondingly Yang and visa - versa for the Yin limbs.

The breathing should also be classified inconjunction with the above into its Yin and Yang elements eg: in relation to martial physical actions when the breath is linked to attacking and advancing, an outward breath is appropriate at the point of striking, which we also class as Yang. On the other hand defensive retreating actions naturally produce an inward breath both being therefore Yin. However in relation to health and soft Qi circulation generally, Yang is now transformed to the inward breath on account the air = Positive Qi coming in, is fresh and therefore good for us. Whilst the outward breath which releases negative Qi now becomes Yin, because if it remains in the lungs and body's cells it is bad for us.

8. *Stand Poised Like a Scale and Move As a Wheel:* The principle behind this maxim, is to help develop cat like balance and reflexes and a sense of roundness. The scale is a piece of equipment that is finely balanced where one half is sensitive to the slightest increase or decrease in weight on the other half. Translated to the human body this means you should always be aware of remaining in a perpetual state of perfect balance, paying particular attention to the hips and shoulders. For when these two areas of the body tilt out of horizontal alignment the rest of the skeletal frame becomes structurally unstable. In moving as a wheel, you need to visualise it in a horizontal and vertical position, then apply it's

properties to the human frame. For example: at the point the wheel touches the floor only a very small portion of it's rim is actually in contact with the ground (called the Point Load). In this upright position it is able to carry a heavy load by distributing a portion of the downward force to the curved outer rim from it's centre. Alternatively in a horizontal position the wheel can create a great force when it acts as a cog transferring the force it generates from it's circular horizontal movement upward or downward or sideways.

You therefore should think of the body as a wheel that when standing with straight legs or squatting into a horse type stance, the rim base is the point where your centre of gravity connects through to the floor via the "Yong Chuan" or "Bubbling Well" cavity, located centrally at the base of the ball of the foot. And the highest point of the wheel rim equates to the "Bai Hui" cavity on the crown of the head. Therefore the "Real DanTien" becomes the "Hub" around which all rotates vertically and horizontally.

From this principle derives the subsidiary maxim of; "Seeking The Straight With The Curve," which basically means for health; Qi will circulate more efficiently through a curved limb or spine than a locked straight limb or spine. And for martial purposes; this feeling of roundness from the wheel creates a buoyancy in the body that lies at the core of the powerful "Peng" skill. Also when pulled or pushed you are able to rotate like the wheel to disrupt your attackers centre and focus.

9. *Apply Your Will (Shen), Not Force:* This is the secret behind the much debated phenomena known as; "Empty Force." That is the ability to move another person without physical contact. From my own point of view I do believe it is possible and although we all have the potential for this, some attune more acutely than others. The only Chinese Tai Chi exponent I personally have witness that was able to demonstrate this to a high level is Master Michael Tse. He on many occasions has rocked not students, but random volunteers from an audience, back and forth from toes to heels, who had no idea what to expect. Achieving this from a distance of up to twenty feet away.

So how does he do it? Well, first you put at least ten years quality Qigong and Tai Chi practice under your belt to develop "Grand Circulation." Then through continued refinement of your Shen and a knowledge of which meridians/cavities to focus on, you arrive at the door of this high level skill. From a martial point of view I doubt if there is any one on the planet who can bounce away a six foot four muscle bound rugby player who has set his heart on dropping you to the ground, without touching him. If however you do touch him, by applying "Peng" the split second you have deflected his charge and directing the soft Jing force with the Shen you should place him onto the seat of his pants.

10. *Seek Serenity In Activity:* This is also known as; "Sung," which is when the body and mind reach the empty stage of development. all distracting thoughts are eliminated and the body becomes light and fully responsive to pure almost subconscious thought waves. It is in this state that the Shen moves unrestricted to direct the Qi to any area of the body, for example: to the hands for healing a patient. Inwardly you have reached a state of "Inner Peace," and feeling of wellbeing continually permeates your bones.

## THE THIRTEEN POSTURES.

These are likewise split into two parts, part one describes the "Eight Gates," that are the key structural components of the Tai Chi postures. And part two comprises of; "Five Steps or Directions," that should operate inconjunction with the "Eight Gates." Combined they form the structure and fabric that is Tai Chi.

### Part One, The Eight Gates.

1. *Ward Off (Peng):* Seen in Fig 29, it is symbolised by "Sky and therefore upward in it's application. It is very Yang in it's usage, eg: Peng charges the arms with Qi or Jing which as the name implies will ward or bounce off all that come into contact with it.

2. *Roll Back ( Lu):* Seen in Fig 30, it is symbolised by "Earth" and is the opposite to Peng as it tends to absorb and direct energy downwards. Very Yin in application, it is the epitome of softness and yielding.

3. *Press (Ghi):* Seen in Fig 31, it is symbolised by "Water" and in application should subtly yet powerfully move like a large swollen river.

Initially it is Yin soft like water, but it's full power Yang, soon makes itself known leaving Yin in its wake.

4. *Push (An):* Seen in Fig 32, it is symbolised by "Fire" which in application and by nature is unpredictable and unstable. Initially you feel it's Yang that disrupts your centre, then within a split second it retreats into Yin leaving you with a false sense of security, a further split second later another and unexpected Yang appears totally destroying your root and centre.

5. *Pull Down (Tsai):* Seen in Fig 39, it is symbolised by "Wind" that starts with Yin as a gentle breeze then from nowhere the destructive and uprooting force of Yang appears, like a gust of wind that lifts off roofs and uproots even the mightiest of trees, bringing them crashing to the ground.

6. *Split (Lieh):* Seen as the transition between Fig 37 and 38, it is symbolised by "Thunder," signifying an initial Yang like a clap of thunder. Again unexpected, it rocks you back on your heels, leaving Yin as the simplest of arm gestures to send you spinning off like a top.

7. *Elbow Strike (Chou):* Seen in Fig 37, it is symbolised by "Lake," whilst all seems calm on the surface, Yin. Beneath the gently lapping waves lies hidden powerful jagged rocks Yang, that smash into and destroys even the sturdiest of ships.

8. *Shoulder Strike (Kao):* Seen in Fig 49, it is symbolised by "Mountain," it is an immovable and powerful obstacle that draws you into it's beauty, Yin. However, If you are racing towards it and suddenly it appears directly in front of you, it will break your bones on its craggy surface, Yang.

**Part Two, The Five Steps.**

9. *Advance:* Seen in Fig 41. As it implies, it involves moving forward with purpose, mentally you should feel as if you are being carried along by a strong current in which all resistance is futile. Martially, if your attacker

decides to retreat he should be made to feel that no matter what he does he cannot escaped you. The distance between you remains constant by your light and fast footwork leaving him feeling a sense of desperation the more he retreats.

10. *Retreat:* Seen in Fig 48. Similar to above only this time it is you who are retreating. The strong current is now pushing you back and martially your attacker feels the distance between you is insurmountable. No matter how fast he travels you always keep one step ahead of him.

11. *Gaze To Left:* Seen in Fig 33, this relates to the principle of using a small force to deflect a larger force. Once this force has been deflected it is sent a great distance. Also it removes you from the line of attack.

12. *Look To The Right:* Seen in Fig 34, it is principally the same as Gaze Left, however in this case you look and follow up with a strike or control technique and take down. Gazing is linked to the Shen which is used to propel someone into the distance.

13. *Central Equilibrium:* Seen in All Fig's, it is the central ridgepole of all Tai Chi postures. The poise balance and grace that sets Tai Chi aside from all other systems are lost if you fail to adhere to this principle. Central equilibrium = Sense of Real Dan Tien + The root of the feet + Postural alignment.

# CHAPTER ELEVEN

# HEALTH BENEFITS OF

# TAI CHI AND QIGONG

The mind and body deeply relax, therefore eliminating the deep rooted tension associated with high blood pressure. Which helps the blood vessels and fine capillaries to dilate, reducing stress on the heart and improves the lung function.

Removes toxins from the joints through regular daily practice of the "Form." Which aligns the skeletal structure to operate in harmony with gravity, thus keeping the forces safely working through the centre of the joints and vital fluids flowing to clear away toxins.

The mental concentration demanded by Tai Chi is believed to stimulate the Cerebral Cortex, helping to rebalance emotions, having a positive effect on the treatment of certain nervous disorders.

The lower abdominal breathing practiced whilst training in Tai Chi has the effect of gently massaging internal organs, which keeps them healthy due to the increased supply of blood to their tissues.

Tai Chi helps break down the fatty tissue through its "Total Body" method of practice, ie: no part of the body is without stimulation, even a small movement will involve every joint, tendon and muscle group thereby eliminating areas of stagnation where fatty deposits will accumulate.

The five senses ie: taste, touch, smell, sight and hearing all receive a boost, due to the increased Qi that circulates through meridians that service these functions and after some years of practice the sixth sense makes itself known.

There is a noticeable change in the immune system that sees the gradual diminishing of the occurrence of bacterial and viral infections that invade the body when we are weak.

Sufferers of stomach complaints such as ulcers or general heartburn will experience a reduction in levels of damaging acids, that cause ulceration and discomfort. The ability to digest food efficiently develops as excess acid levels drop.

Those who suffer from asthma will see a reduction in the frequency of attacks as stress levels drop and Lung/Bronchial function improves. Subtle opening and closing of the chest keeps the lungs full of Qi and ensures all areas (especially the lower third) are motorised with every inward and outward breath. Which differs from how we normally breath ie: high in the chest more commonly known as shallow breathing.

Skin tone and texture improves as Qi levels build in the body. It is said regular practice of Tai Chi strengthens the Wei Qi (outer protective energy) as well as the Nei Qi (inner energy). It is this Wei Qi distributed evenly across the skin that attracts an increased supply of blood to the tissues giving it it's healthy sheen.

The Chinese call the spirit; "Shen," when someone is in the peak of health and fitness they have strong Shen. When the Shen is low it usually accompanies sadness or ill health. Therefore a disciplined approach to regularly practice Tai Chi noticeably raises the Shen to a constant level, that keeps the emotions in check and strengthens the immune system.

There will be an interesting increase in stamina, not just in the length of time you can sustain exercise, but also in mental powers or the period of time you can stay mentally focussed. The Qi reserves that build up and are stored in the lower abdomen, not only feed the muscles and tendons but, also support the brains functions over long periods of usage, which is when fatigue usually kicks in.

Regular practice clears out the Jinglou or energy pathways, likened to dredging of a river which then facilitates the free flow of the water (Qi). This process is created by a combination of subtle posture movements and Taoist breathing.

Tests in China have discovered that Tai Chi and Qigong increases the white and red bloodcell count. Also the protein levels of the red cells increase nourishing the organs and leaving you with a sense of well being.

Lifting the head as if suspended by a string from above whilst drooping the buttocks, releases the hypertonic muscles that misalign the pelvis and spine when the posture is poor.

Standing in Horse Stance (Ma Bu), is beneficial in the relief of constipation.

When the Qi is sunk to the Dan Tien, the spleen, stomach and whole digestive tract will work more efficiently.

Synovial fluid flows around the joints when practicing Tai Chi, this effectively washes out the toxins into the blood stream leaving the joints clean and healthy.

Tai Chi assists the lymphatic fluids to flow throughout the system, thus increasing the potential for detoxification of the body.

The Endocrine (Glandular) system produces chemicals called hormones which are secreted directly into the blood stream. In conjunction with the nervous system these hormones control the internal environment of the body. Tai Chi and Qigong works directly on this system keeping it healthy, flowing and balanced.

Tai Chi and Qigong are the complete health and fitness package, that offers inner and outer protection to the many obstacles that are placed across our paths, that would otherwise shorten our journey through life. It therefore provides a safe passageway into longevity, returning us to the source relatively unscathed.

# CHAPTER TWELVE

# QUESTIONS AND ANSWERS

Over the years I have been confronted with a multitude of questions from newcomers to Tai Chi and Qigong. So I thought it appropriate to list them with their corresponding answers for the benefit of those who are about to join our ranks.

Q: What should I wear?

A: Generally loose fitting cloths eg: baggy T Shirt and jogging bottoms. And for the feet, comfy flat shoes or none at all.

Q: What age group is it best suited for ?

A: I always say eight to eighty and even outside those parameters for special cases.

Q: Will this training help my health problem ?

A: I generalised this question because the plain answer is yes, as Tai Chi and Qigong helps relieve a multitude of ailments. However, it is also important you understand it is not a panacea for everyone. Like everything else in life if you don't invest, you won't get the returns.

Q: Is it a religion or linked to religious beliefs ?

A: The plain and simple answer to both points is a resounding; No!

It is purely and simply a health science and martial art.

Q: Do I have to learn it as a block course ?

A: No, though some do link it to a six or twelve week introductory programme, in the main it is taught with an open door policy.

Q: How often should I practice ?

A: For the first six months, ten to fifteen minutes a day is adequate. Thereafter you can gradually build up to anything from half an hour to one and a half hours per day depending on your age, abilities or commitments.

Q: Where should I practice ?

A: The same basic principles apply as stated in chapter nine in regards of location, but I will add a rider : outdoors at all times if possible, subject to the weather conditions.

Q: Should I continue to train with a cold or flu ?

A: Depending on how you feel, with a cold you should curtail your usual workout to a short and very light programme. But with the flu rest is advised supplemented by meditation only, also for a short period.

Q: I am disabled and in a wheelchair, could I take up these arts ?

A: Yes of course you can, you can benefit greatly from the "Tai Chi and Qigong, Head to Toe Programme" I have devised specially for a seated position.

Q: I practice another martial art, will Tai Chi clash with it in any way ?

A: No, to the contrary, Tai Chi does nothing but enhance your martial potential by internalising whatever style you practice.

Q: Is yoga compatible with Tai Chi and Qigong ?

A: Yes most styles of yoga can be practiced along side these arts, however there are a few dynamic yoga styles that may become confused and therefore I suggest you consult your yoga teacher in this instance.

Q: I train hard every day at my local fitness studio and play squash twice a week, why should I need to take up Tai Chi or Qigong ?

A: Read my book!

Q: How would I recognise a good teacher ?

A: Does he or she look, sound and smell healthy? Has he or she trained for at least ten years linked to a recognised master ? Do his /her existing students look healthy and in fine spirits ? If the answer to all the above is yes, you've found one.

Q: How do I qualify as a teacher ?

A: I would suggest you join a school that is registered with either: The Tai Chi Union For Great Britain or The British Council For Chinese Martial Arts (check out the Web) and enrol on their teachers training programme.

Q: How long will it take me to learn the form ?

A: As I've stated earlier in this book , this depends on
your instruction absorption rate and how much commitment
you can give to your training.  But as a general guide,
you should allow six to twelve months for the "Short
Form," and eighteen months to two years for the "Long Form."

Q: Will it help me increase my chances of conceiving a baby ?

A: Yes I was actually asked this question and I answered by
reassuring her that Tai Chi and Qigong are designed to
rebalance us externally and internally therefore it's got to
be of some benefit.

Q: Should I become pregnant, can I continue to practice ?

A: Yes , I highly recommend it to keep you supple through to
the end of the nine months.  Although from between seven
and eight months you my find it somewhat restrictive.
The relaxation methods and deep refreshing abdominal
breathing we teach is particularly useful in the final run up
to the birth.

# CHAPTER THIRTEEN

# APPENDIX

**Acknowledgments.**

I would like to state my love and deep gratitude to my wife Lesley who has supported me and has always been my rock.

I want to thank my children Janine and Richard for their patience, love and understanding.

Thanks to Darryl Moy for all his useful suggestions and help.

A special thanks to: Pete, Mike, Celia, Steve, Hilary, Dave, Maureen, Ann, Kieth, Yve, Mike, Gunilla, Gabrialla, Phil, Richard, Romey, Sally, Debbie, Rob, Mark, Martin, Ann, Linda, Janet, Pete, Sue, Ruth, Phil, Pauline, Jeff, Eirian, Barbara, Mary, Janine, Lisa, Mum and Carli, Caroline and Maureen and all my other students who support me in my research.

To the three masters who have and still do inspire me to continue on this incredible journey: Masters Chu, Tse and Yang.

Peter Newton
October 2000.

**Six Qigong - Foundation Exercises.**

1. *Swinging The Arms Whilst Bouncing:* Relaxes the shoulders elbows and wrists. Helps develop a sense of energy wave from the spine to the hands. Acts as a general invigorator.

2. *Holding The Qi Ball Whilst Twisting:* Alternately stimulates and exercises the muscles of the lower back. Gently separates the vertebra of the spine to release blockage and pressure on the joints.

3. *Advance and Retreat "Tai Chi Waist Exercise:"* Therapy for constipation and general stiffness in lower back and hips. Helps develop the "Qua" or deeply sunk hip movements of Tai Chi.

4. *One Hand Up, One Hand Down Tai Chi Coordination:* Unites and coordinates all joints, tendons and muscle groups of the body. Develops the smooth "Silk Reeling Energy" of the body unique to Tai Chi.

5. *Bending, Twisting, Stretching and Tilting:* Increases flexibility in the spine. Exercises all the key muscles of the torso. Improves the Qi (oxygenated and nutrient carrying blood) supply to all the organs.

6. *Monkey Breathing:* Improves and strengthens the lung function. Clears the head from negative thoughts and Qi that can trigger stress related symptoms and migraine headaches.

**Six Qigong Exercises - Level One.**

1. *Tai Chi Symbol Figure Eight:* Strengthens lower back and abdominal muscles. Stimulates kidneys and develops Qi spiral in torso and arms.

2. *Open and Closing The Arms:* Strengthen both cardiovascular and respiratory systems by opening and closing the chest cavity.

3. *Lifting and Lowering The Heels:* Therapy for prostate, haemorrhoid and legs circulation problems. Stimulates the cerebral cortex.

4. *Crane Swoops Down and Stretches The Spine:* Stretches the spine. Stimulates and gently massages the kidneys and generally strengthens the spine Qi.

5. *Gather The Heavenly Qi and Swing Through The Legs:* As number two but also strengthens all key torso muscles and kidneys.

6. *Tai Chi Breathing:* Trains natural and Taoist breathing methods. Develops Grand Circulation.

**37 Posture Classical Yang Style Tai Chi Chuan Form.**

*Foundation:*

1. Tai Chi Beginning. ( Tai Chi Che Shih).

2. Grasp The Birds Tail. (Lan Chiao Wei).

3. Single Whip. (Tan Pien).

4. Lifting Hands and Step Up. (Ti Shou Shang Shih).

5. White Crane Airs Wings. (Pai Hao Liang Chih).

6. Brush Knee and Press. (Tso Lou Hsih).

7. Play The Pi Pa. (Shou Hui Pi Pa).

8. Brush Knee and Twist Step. (Tso Lou Hsih Au Bu).

9. Deflect Down Parry and Punch. (Chin Pu Lan Chui).

10. As If Shut Up. (Yu Feng Shih Pi).

11. Embrace Tiger and Return To Mountain. (Pao Hu Kuei Shan).

*Part One:*

12. Grasp The Birds Tail.

13. Single Whip (Part only).

14. Seeing Fist Under Elbow. (Chou Ti Kan Chui).

15. Backstepping Monkey. (Tso Tao Nien Hou).

16. Diagonal Flight. (Hsieh Fei Shih).

17. Wave Hands Like Clouds. (Yuen Shou).

18. Single Whip.

19. Lower The Snake Body. (She Shen Hsia Shih).

20. Golden Cock Stands On One Leg. (Chin Chi Tu Li).

21. Stand High To Examine The Horse. (Kan T'an Ma).

22. Separate Right and Left. (Yu Fen Chiao).

23. Turn and Kick With Heel. (Chuan Shen Teng).

24. Brush Knee and Twist Step.

*Part Three:*

25. Step Up and Punch Down. (Chin Pu Tsai Ch'ui).

26. Grasp The Birds Tail.

27. Single Whip.

28. Fair Lady Weaves Shuttle. (Yu Nu Ch'uan Suo).

29. Grasp The Birds Tail.

30. Single Whip.

31. Lower The Snake Body.

32. Step Forward To Seven Stars. (Shang Pu Ch'i Hsing).

33. Step Back and Ride The Tiger. ( T'ui Pu K'ua Fu).

34. Turn Body and Sweep Lotus With Leg. (Chuan Shen Pai Lien).

35. Draw The Bow and Shoot The Tiger. (Wan Kung She Fu).

36. Deflect Down Parry and Punch.

37. As If Shut Up.

38. Embrace Tiger and Return To Mountain.

39. Close Tai Chi. (Ho Tai Chi).

# Master Tse Teaches Chen Form.

# Broadsword Training With
# Master Yang Jwing Ming.

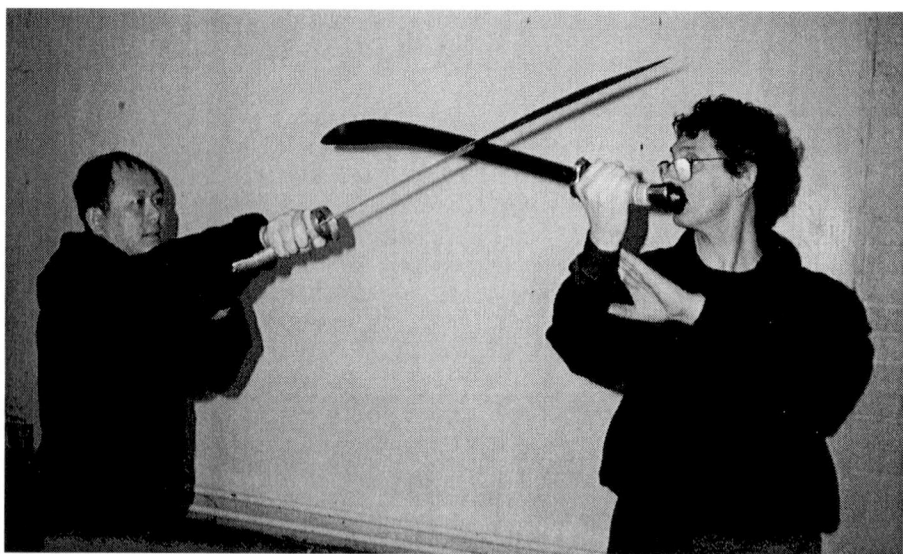

**Pushing Hands With Master Yang.**

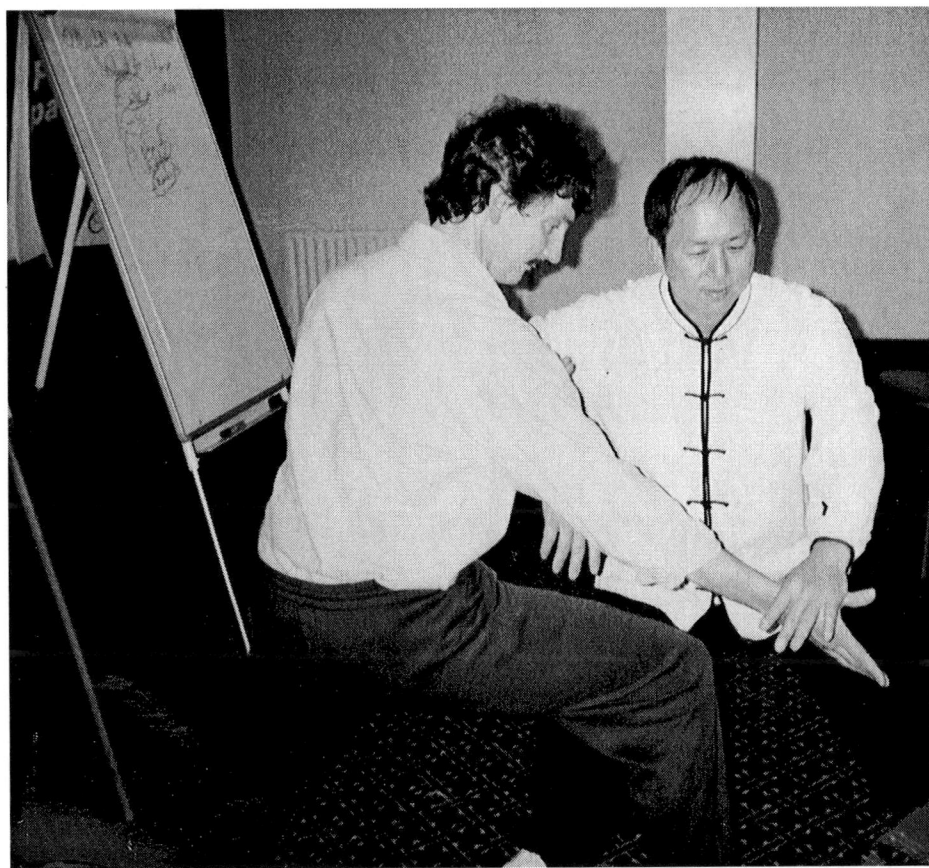